I0456098

Rising Dawn :
Demons of mental
illness defeated

Rising Dawn :
Demons of mental illness defeated

Margret David

Copyright © 2011 by Margret David.

Library of Congress Control Number: 2011900722
ISBN: Hardcover   978-1-4568-5323-5
                       Softcover   978-1-4568-5322-8
                       Ebook   978-1-4568-5324-2

All rights reserved. No part of this book may be reproduced or transmitted in any form or by any means, electronic or mechanical, including photocopying, recording, or by any information storage and retrieval system, without permission in writing from the copyright owner.

This is a true story. Names, characters, and places have been changed or not mentioned for confidentiality purposes.

This book was printed in the United States of America.

To order additional copies of this book, contact:
Xlibris Corporation
0-800-644-6988
www.xlibrispublishing.co.uk
Orders@xlibrispublishing.co.uk
301370

FOREWORD

I dedicate this book to Matthew, Melody, MacDonald, Constance, Neddy, Winfred, Geraldine, and Anderson for all the love and support they showed me through the dark hours.

A special thanks to Pastor Ivy, Pastor Emmanuel, and Susan for all their prayers and support in difficult times.

To Elisha Goodman, Thank you very much for being such a wonderful and committed prayer coach.

To Dr Morris Cerullo, Kenneth, and Gloria Copeland, thank you for the literature you send me which has helped me gain a deeper understanding of the things of God.

To all the pastors on God channel, Wonderful TV, TBN, Word Network, LOVEWORLD, and all gospel channels, thank you for enriching my spirit.

May God bless you all.

INTRODUCTION

In the month of October 2010, I had a dream. In the dream, there was a man preaching and healing people. I went to the man and asked him to heal me of this thing that kept coming up from my stomach to block my throat. The man first ignored me, and when I asked for the second time, he turned round and faced me. He smiled and said to me, 'Read the books and you will be complete.' When I woke up, I remembered the dream so vividly, and I knew God had spoken to me. I was being asked to read the Bible. I had read the Bible many times, only this time it was going to be different. A great revelation of my past, which had been for a long time the roots of my problems, was going to be revealed. The issues that had troubled my life for a long time were going to be exposed.

This was a time in my life when I was weary in flesh and in spirit. I had questions that I needed God to answer. I needed a spiritual uplifting which I wasn't getting in my church. The Word of God was so shallow, and praying was so limited. I felt that my spirit wasn't fed enough and that somehow I was not going to get what I was looking for. Although I continued praying at home, I desperately wanted to leave my church. I wasn't getting the answers I wanted from the word that was being preached. I had lived in a marriage where I had suffered domestic violence for more than fifteen years. Now the actual physical aggression was gone but the hate, despise, and hostility was still there. I had no doubt that God was watching over me but why was I with a man who didn't care for me or our children. His relatives were even worse, stealing everything we worked for. They had stolen our lives, our children's future and inheritance. Honestly, couldn't God see what I was going through? He has all the power to make my life better, then, why has it taken him so long? I had prayed for this marriage for seventeen years, but nothing changed until I had turned round to God and said, 'The prayers I have made concerning this marriage are enough. I am not going to make any more prayers again concerning this marriage. If you have heard my prayers and have not acted in these seventeen years, so be it. You shall act when you want to, but when you do, let your will be done.' Five years later, I was still experiencing the same but this time I was demanding an audience with him. Nothing would satisfy me unless he spoke to me and answered me face to face. I was not taking no for an answer. God answers in mysterious ways; he took me on a journey of my life, opening my eyes to many things that had not meant a thing to me yet they were the roots of what was happening to me. What I was going to experience is what I have written in this book. It was a painful healing process.

At work, things weren't any better. There was so much physical and verbal aggression going on, racial abuse, and a lot of antagonism. I did not understand why I was working with the violent mentally ill when my father promised that he will prosper me. My father promised me peace and prosperity yet here I was in a violent environment. I began to question God why for three years I was working in a dangerous environment with clients who were so aggressive and unpredictable, which was the same thing I had experienced in my marriage. Why did God have to put me in violent situations all the time? I was not a child from a violent kingdom. Why as a child of God, who possesses everything, was I found to be struggling for a better peaceful job? Was being in violent situations ever going to end in my life? What I did not realise was that God had protected me in that environment for more than three years for the reason that was going to be revealed to me.

CHAPTER 1

Let me tell you about my work. In the first year of work after graduating as a mental health nurse, I started working in a low secure forensic hospital. I was working with men and women who were suffering from mental illness and had learning disabilities problems as well. Some of them had committed crimes, such as arson, attempted murder, murder, stabbings, violent assaults on people, sexual crimes, and were detained in hospital for treatment. A few had life sentences while others had indefinite sentences. Then there were those who had been sexually abused, assault victims, depressed, bereaved, those who had become mentally ill due to taking drugs, and those who had a history of mental illness in their families. Their state of the mind had been given as a reason as to why they had committed the crimes they were detained for.

These are the people that no one wants to work with. As I strongly believe that Jesus lives in me and the Holy Spirit is in me and upon me all the time, I could not understand why Jesus and the Holy Spirit being in me could let me work in this environment and not change my situation to give me a better job. What I saw in my job was beyond belief. Women and men were being tormented by evil spirits in unbelievable ways. Everything was put down to medicine and science. Anyone working in my profession is not allowed to exercise their faith in their place of work; therefore, when you saw an attack, you were not allowed to pray for the client. You are not allowed by law to introduce Jesus to these people. Church people could come if they got the permission but there was hardly any coming. During my three years of practice, only once did I see a Roman Catholic priest coming to pray for one of the clients.

During my second year of work, the Holy Spirit started to reveal things to me. I started to learn more about these people's life experiences. In more than three quarters of the situations, these people had suffered abuse in their childhood, some of it horrific. They had grown into adults with a troubled past and never known how to deal with their feelings from the past. Violence controls their lives. When they attack, they have so much strength, and they aim to hurt people and to kill. Sometimes the attacks would go for days, and everyone would be saying, 'Oh, that one is possessed.' This was because the behaviour that the person will be exhibiting would be shocking and inhumane. The following are some of the behaviours I have witnessed associated with the violence:

Hostility towards everyone

Urinating on themselves deliberately

Defecating and throwing faeces at people

Hitting out at people

Pulling people's hair out

Scratching people

Throwing items at people

Ripping bathroom sinks and taps

Breaking window handles and using them as weapons

Breaking glass or light bulbs and using them as weapons

Breaking windows

Kicking doors in

Threatening to kill using knives

Holding people hostage with a biro pen held to their neck

Inserting batteries into their bowel through the anal system

Picking skin to make wounds on themselves

Slashing wrists with glass, plastic, or razors

Causing lacerations to their bodies

Overturning tables at meal times

Throwing chairs at others

Pouring hot drinks on themselves or others

Threatening to stab people with broken pieces of bathroom sinks

Refusing to bath, eat, or drink

Eating sanitary pads they had used for their monthly periods

Standing on top of a TV in the lounge and urinating there

Head butting walls and doors

Punching walls and doors

Fighting one another

Attempting suicide with shoe laces, bras, ties on clothes, and anything available

Attempting to strangle others

Uncommunicative

Unreasonable

Refusing to eat

Attempting to run away

Rocking with heads facing down

Refusing to sleep, and this can go on for days

During the time the person is free from the attack; the person appears sane, reasonable, and can have a good adult conversation with you. During the attack, they become a very different person, uncommunicative, very difficult to reason with, very violent and aggressive.

There is a lot more that happened. When a patient came into hospital, there seemed to be an escalation of the behaviours. When they came in expressing one set of behaviours, they soon had more, usually what they saw others doing, and this was explained as copied behaviour but the fact is, the behaviours were escalating. If this is copied behaviour, then how do we explain what they were admitted for? Is it copied as well?

My question to God was, if the Lord Jesus said,

> I have given you authority over all power of the enemy and you can walk among snakes and crush them. Nothing will injure you. But don't rejoice because evil spirits obey you. Rejoice because your names are registered in heaven (Luke 10:18).

If the church was given this power, where is it in all this? These are the people in desperate need of deliverance by the power given by Jesus Christ, but these are to the very people who are hidden in mental health hospitals, in prisons, and are completely hidden to the world of Christianity. The law has even effectively shut those who are Christians working in these environments from exercising their faith. What is the point of me working where I am not allowed to exercise my faith or even offer comforting words from the Bible? These are the souls that need that redemption mostly because they are in true darkness. These are souls completely lost to the world. It did not make any sense to me, and it pained me to see how these people suffered. There are so many interpretations to mental illness. There are scientific explanations, biological and social explanations. The diagnosis is mainly centred on the behaviours expressed. When these are grouped together, they usually give a diagnosis. However, as I was reading from Genesis, reading verses 1:28 and 2:7, the word of the Lord came to me saying,

> When I formed man in his mother's womb, I gave him a clean
> spirit which was breathed into him directly from me. That spirit
> is part of me. It carries my joy, power, anointing and it is my
> presence in a human being.

I then realised that if God gave everyone his spirit, then mental illness is an attack from the devil to destroy what God had planted in man. But why did God let that happen. I looked at my situation and said, 'God, why would you let someone torment anyone's spirit. These people have been abused in many different ways in their past and ever since they have been tormented. What happened to them? Did it change the chemistry in their bodies? Did it damage their brains? What exactly happened in them? They have no rest in their lives. What about me; I am not locked up but I have been abused and have been a prisoner in my own home for a long time. Why has this abuse not damaged me to the extent of being locked up?

CHAPTER 2

Domestic Violence

My life had not been too good. I suffered domestic violence for a long time. I still held the pain in me. I had been humiliated, physically and verbally abused, ridiculed, and made to feel worthless, bullied, harassed, threatened, and nearly strangled to death. I found it very hard *to* let go. I was still bitter. One day, I came across the following scripture:

> But the lord in his holy temple, the lord, still rules from heaven.
> Examining every person on earth. The lord examines both the
> righteous and the wicked. He hates those who love violence.

This scripture tells us that nothing escapes the eyes of God. He knows everyone, and nothing even the tiniest thing is hidden from his sight. Perpetrators of domestic violence usually abuse their victims in private; they do not want the world to know. In public, they appear very polite, sincere, and are very likeable that most people won't believe when told about how they behave. No matter how they hide it, God still sees it. It is clearly said that God *hates* violence. The word *hates* indicates that this is a serious matter with God. He does not like it at all.

I was a victim of domestic violence for more than fifteen years. I had no freedom in my life. I couldn't do what I wanted to do without my husband's permission. I thought I had found a husband who would love and care for me but I had found someone who was going to abuse me for a long time. I had met my husband Cavin through a family friend, who recommended that he was a good man. Although I was educated and had a good job and a good salary, I was never able to do anything counted. My husband was determined to see all my plans, my thoughts, and anything I tried to do, go down the drain. He financially abused me. With my earnings, I had to provide food for the family, childcare, clothing for my children, and pay for their education. The only thing that my children got from their father was payment for their medical bills because this was paid for by his company where he worked. This meant he had all his money to himself. Cavin had a son of his own from a previous relationship who was staying with us. When there was no food in the house or when he felt the food wasn't good enough, he would go and buy takeaway and ate with my stepson while my daughter and I looked. When I was pregnant with my second child, Cavin would take the food I was eating and give it to my stepson even when I had not had enough. He did this despite his son having his own share. I was the one bringing the food in the house but denied the right to have enough. Whenever I was broke and asked him to help, he refused and was abusive.

Beef was very expensive then, and whenever I cooked a vegetarian meal, I got beaten up for it. He called it rubbish food. Then he would go and buy a piece of beef, cook it, and eat with my stepson while my daughter and I looked. He wanted beef every day, and he would not buy it. If he bought it, he would bring the receipt and asked me to pay him all the money he had used. I remember one day I got beaten up and bruised all over for not affording to pay fees for my stepson. It was difficult as I also had to pay fees for my daughter's nursery, buy uniforms, and pay for childcare. The burden of looking after my stepson had been put on me as well. I was criticised for everything I did and was told that I was going to amount to nothing. He compared me with all our women neighbours and said they were all better than me. He flirted with women in front of me and showed no remorse at all. My life was controlled and very unhappy. I was unhappy in my own home, and I never enjoyed what I worked for. At family gatherings, I was ridiculed in front of his relatives, and he enjoyed talking down to me. He had no respect for me whatsoever.

Cavin's family was so much involved in consulting spirit mediums in whatever they did. Their lives were run by witch doctors and their witchcraft activities. Out of the eight children in his family, Cavin and his eldest sister Bev were the only ones working. Cavin paid for all the bills for the spirit medium consultations, witch doctors, and the ceremonies they were asked to do. The ceremonies were very expensive to do but they were often told that after performing these ceremonies, their problems would go away and they would become very rich. They never got rich, and their problems still remained. If all that money would have been put to good use, we probably could be wealthy today. My children and I were deprived from the very beginning from what God had allocated to our lives.

One day a friend of mine who worked with Bev came to me and said, 'Do you know that your husband comes every month to our place of work to give your sister-in-law some money?' My friend was aware of my situation, and she felt sorry for me. Cavin earned more than I did but his wages were never used in our home. I could see receipts of groceries he bought for Bev. Cavin never gave me money to spend on food, myself, or to spend on the children. Of all the twenty-two years I lived with him, there was never a day that he gave me cash to go and do my own shopping. I never received presents, birthday cards, Christmas cards, flowers, chocolates, or anything even to say thank you for the laundry, cleaning, or cooking I did for him. I have worked and looked after myself and my children. Cavin and his family were told by the spirit medium that going to church was useless. It did not make anyone rich. They were told it was like burying your problems yet they remained bothering you. I was later to discover what this means. They were told that they were rich people and that they were going to make a lot of money, which of course they never made. They were given some concussions to use and asked to perform ceremonies, but they never made the money. I had grown in a Christian family, attended church every Sunday, and I had spend four years of my education at a catholic school, being taught good morals and about God. I refused to obey the things Cavin said the spirit mediums had told them. This rebellion cost me my peace. I simply didn't believe in them, for I always felt they were lying. I could not find a place for them in my heart. Bev invited the spirit mediums into their father's house to stay with them, and they were consulting them every day on all the issues of their lives. They influenced Cavin that if I did not listen to him and do what he wanted, he should hit me to make me listen and obey him. Here was a man taking the place of God, wanting another human being created by God to obey him when he himself was not obeying God. Obeying him would have meant obeying the ways of the devil he was following. If he had been obeying God and acting according to God's word, I would have obeyed him for I would have known in my heart that God was right with him. Bev actually made a statement that Cavin was never going to achieve anything as long as he had me as a wife.

When the devil walks into your life and settles in your house, it is like you are living in hell. Your cheeks are always wet with tears. I know now that I was being used by someone to pay his bills, to feed his family, to satisfy his sexual needs, and was being abused on top of that. Indirectly, I was also used to pay the bills for their witch doctor consultations, ceremonies, and to feed his relatives because he was using me to take care of his responsibilities to his advantage. This was someone who didn't care about me at all. He was happy to keep me there as long as he achieved what he and his relatives wanted. I was blind then; I could not see the gravity of my situation. I give thanks to God now for he has kept me through all. The devil had come to destroy my destiny and my path. I had been brought up an intelligent girl, who had opportunities to become wealthy and huge. Here I was, oblivious of what was going on in my life. I could not see the light. Whenever I ran away, Cavin would come to take me back and my relatives would encourage me to go back. My church was against divorce and here I was stuck in hell. Twice I tried to commit suicide but what stopped me was the idea of leaving my daughter with these people. I could see that my daughter would have no one to pay fees for her, clothe her, or even have enough to eat. This man was using me to do the work God had given him to do. I thank God now more than ever because I know that whatsoever the devil has stolen away from me, he shall pay it back with interest. (Lev. 6:1-7)

The abuser will try to isolate you from everyone, your friends, family, and everything that matters to you. What the devil will be trying to do is to make you lose your mind. You become isolated, depressed, worried, and tormented in spirit. You wonder what you have done wrong. You are not free even in what you say; you become more aware of your actions, fearing that you will upset your abuser. Cavin was having affairs with other women and people told me. One day, I saw a pair of worn out ladies knickers in the drawers of our bed, and I confronted him but he denied any knowledge of them. I had been away for a few days, and he had stayed behind in the house on his own. The violence and verbal abuse continued. My parents had separated when I was fifteen years, and he used to say abuses directed at my parents because of their separation. He said, 'I had parents who had separated and that I was going to be like them because I always wanted to leave him.' My sister-in-law at one time told Cavin to leave me and take my children away from me and give them to her to look after. This was a way of her trying to get more money from Cavin as she would be claiming that she needed the money for the needs of the children. Why would a woman want to look after another woman's children when the mother of the children is alive and capable? I praise God because I have done a good job with my children through his power, and God has provided for them the way Bev could never have done. Bev even told Cavin that my daughter was not going to achieve anything in life; she was going to be a problem to us. She was always with spirit mediums, telling her about other people's lives but the devil is a liar. God has proved her and her witch doctors liars.

Every time you feel like you are sinking deeper and deeper into the hands of your abuser. You start to see no way out. I was not going to church at this time. Cavin discouraged me from going to church. Although I was not going to church, there was something in my spirit that kept me going. I had such a strong resistive spirit within me, and my spirit was always fighting. I realise now that it was part of the spirit of God within me that refused to die. It lived despite all what happened. I just did not know how to activate it into action. I had no idea what I was dealing with. I was completely ignorant of the powers of the devil that were operating in my life. Everyone in the neighbourhood knew my situation; some sympathised with me and some laughed when I walked past. I had lost my dignity but still I kept going. When you are in such a situation, people treat you like nothing. Despite my struggles, my pain and torment, Bev hated me and accused me of being mean when she was the one who was getting money from Cavin. Getting money that was meant for our family. She wanted me to give her the money I was earning as well. She hated me for what I earned with my sweat and blood. At least I was earning honest money, and she was stealing from my family by saying bad things about me so that she would win Cavin on her side and get money out of him. She would make comments such as they have a lot of money because there are two of them working and that we eat good food while she was struggling. She did not even want me to enjoy my hard work. She was jealous of my life and fought hard to make me live miserably. She forgot that she was the one getting money from Cavin, robbing my family of our God-given earnings, while I was left to struggle with running the household all by myself. The house Cavin and I got together, I was told it wasn't mine despite paying for the foundation, the roof, and other building materials. I was cut off from the house. When I moved to another country, Bev moved into the house and now posses the house. She has refused to leave the house and has declared that she will not move, and Bev is now in charge of the house. It now belongs to Bev. She now lives in the house; she has put some lodgers in the house and collects rentals every month which she uses to look after herself. I was tricked and used to build a house for other people. My husband tricked me into believing that the house was for us and the children; never did I know that he and Bev were using me to make their ends meet. What does God say about my sweat and blood? Where is God's fairness and justice in all this? When it came to signing the papers for the house, one of my brothers-in-law told Cavin to sign the papers on his own so that if he wanted to divorce me, he could still keep the house and marry another woman. That is how I have lost what I worked for; my sweat and blood gone; my children's inheritance gone in the wind. That's how the abuse got so bad. I was abused by Cavin and his eldest sister.

When I used the extended part of the house as a pre-school and for after-school classes, helping other children with their work as I was teacher, I was made to pay a third of the income I got from my extra work to Cavin as rentals. What was left in my pocket was only enough to pay the teachers who assisted me, the cleaner, and buy food for the pre-school children. I made no profit at all. I held three jobs at the time; my teaching job in government earned enough to keep my household running. When I started our pre-school, we were using a small stove. It was okay in the beginning as we had few children in the pre-school. As the numbers grew, I bought a bigger stove. On the day it was delivered, Cavin took the stove outside at night and said he did not want it in the house as he said I had bought it without telling him. There was a great risk of it being stolen, so one of our neighbours took it and put in his house for safe keeping. He later agreed to have the stove back in the house after that neighbour had pleaded with him. Cavin later sold that stove without my knowledge and never gave me penny out of it. One day I got paid from my government job, Cavin asked if I could lend him some money to buy a battery for his minibus. I explained to him that I did not have any money, the only money I had was for food. He said he would use the food money and replace it the following week. When the time came and I asked for the money, he said he didn't have it. I had children in the house that needed food, and I knew he had been paid and he had money. When I told him that he had to get me some money because there was no food in the house, I was strangled until I was choking and foaming in the mouth. My children panicked, and they ran to seek help from a neighbour. My neighbour came and tried to diffuse the situation. He denied having strangled me.

One day salvation came through a friend of mine. She sympathised with my situation and invited me for a prayer meeting. She taught me how to pray. Every day she took me up a mountain to a place of prayer. She prayed in tongues, and I did not understand anything about tongues. She taught me about fasting, and one day she said, 'God has told me that you are ready to receive tongues. I am going to pray for you, and you will receive the gift today.' She then said, 'If you feel like saying something even if it doesn't mean anything to you, just say it, those are tongues.' When she prayed, nothing happened. I went home and that night as I was praying before going to bed, the spirit of the Lord descended upon me, and I started to speak in tongues. There was this warmth that came into me, so beautiful and fulfilling; I felt so much at peace within myself. My life changed in so many ways. Somehow the spirit within me started to grow to become bigger than the situation. My fight had just begun. Two weeks after giving birth to my second child, Bev brought her seriously ill younger sister into my house for me to look after while I was still poorly myself. She said the spirit mediums had told them that she could not stay at their father's house because there were many evil spirits at that house. I thought she was being cruel and being a bully. Cavin never said anything. This was a man who was supposed to take care and protect me being told what to do by his sister and not caring what impact that would have on his wife's health. They left their sister in my care when I also had a newly born baby to look after. She needed personal care, bathing, feeding, and lifting. Every woman who has given birth would know and tell that this is not the best of the times to be doing all that hard work. From that time, I started suffering back problems. Even in that situation, I prayed every day, and I even prayed the last prayer for Bev's sister she died in my house. I m still alive today to tell my story; that's how faithful my God has been for me. He has kept me through all the cruelty.

One day when Cavin wanted to hit me, something just gripped me from within, and I stood up with so much strength and courage and I shouted, 'Devil, you are not going to touch me today in Jesus's name!' I kept shouting the same words over and over again, and Cavin just fled the house.

The spirit of domestic violence is one that carries the demons of pain. It causes pain to everyone who is at the receiving end. There is pain to the physical flesh and pain that eats one inside especially from knowing that this has been perpetrated by someone close to you. The same person who is supposed to show you love treats you with so much hate that you see them wishing you dead and even attempting to murder you, and the church still think you do not have to divorce. Is that what God wants for his children? Is that what Jesus died for? To be slaves to other people. How can the church justify this? My church still tells me I don't have to divorce. They do not live my life, I do. I am the one who is being abused. I clean, cook, do laundry, pay bills, provide food yet I still get beaten up, get degraded, abused, and humiliated. A person in my situation would feel low in spirit, confused because you wonder what wrong you have done. In the case of Cavin, this was someone I was supposed to trust, yet he was so hurtful, never mind his relatives with their influence. Where does that leave one's mindset? You become anxious around him, even when you are in the same bed with him, you feel abused, betrayed, and filthy, and it builds hostility in you. This is the place where the devil wants you. Like any condition that causes illness to the body, this causes illness to the mind. This becomes an open door for the spirit of hate to enter. You start hating him in retaliation, despise him with every vein in your body, you want revenge, and you become hostile. If not careful you even want to murder them. You lose your faith and trust in them. You plan how to react in situations when you get attacked. You even start to hide weapons for defending yourself. You start to become cold and calculating in your actions to save your own skin. You want to do something that will make them never lay a figure on you ever again. My situation was made worse by the fact that Cavin was a policeman and the law concerning domestic violence was not good at that time. I tried reporting him once, but more beatings followed after that. In my line of work, I have come across women suffering from anxiety disorders and posttraumatic stress due to what has been done to them. Some have gone to prison because the way they have retaliated has been too extreme, causing grievous bodily harm or even death. That's how bad it becomes. Some who have not had the courage to retaliate have committed suicide.

CHAPTER 3

How I Coped

Before I came to know Jesus, I used to tell my mother what was happening, but it was very difficult as I could see it was all so painful for her. Sometimes, she would cry and hated Cavin and Bev for their actions towards me. I had friends I could talk to. When I received Jesus, I found it quite easier to say everything in prayer as I believed someone was listening to me until one day when in a dream, a very tall man, the size of two six feet man, whose body was all hairy like a beast, said to me, 'Do you want to know what God looks like?' I said yes. He said, 'Look behind you.' The light that I saw was extraordinary. It was extremely bright, even brighter than the sun on its brightest day. You could not even look at it twice or blink in it. It covered the heavens and the earth, and it was so powerful. It can never be compared to anything in brightness and power. I quickly bowed my head and was on my knees instantly. When I woke up, I knew beyond any doubt that God was real. I became very convinced that there was a very powerful God who was hearing my prayers and who had so much power that no darkness would stand in his presence. That God wanted me to know him. I never looked back. My God had come to reassure me that he truly existed. I would pour out my heart to God in hard times. My life changed *to* more. I knew that taking refuge in my God was like taking refuge in a power and strength that would never be accessible to any evil.

The reason I did not have a mental breakdown is because I had found Jesus, and the Lord revealed himself to me. He was my hiding place. I found comfort in knowing that he was there for me no matter what. I read the Bible and verses like, Isaiah 49:16, 'See I have written your name on the palm of my hand.' I knew if my name was curved on the palm of God's hand, I was special to him, why else would my name be written on God's hand. If he who created the world loved me so much to make it a point that my name does not go out of his sight, then he must care enough and watch over me.

When I saw the vision of God in the dream and felt the power of the light, I surely knew that no evil would ever stand in the presence of the Lord. The force in his presence would just send any evil down on its knees. I was reassured of a power and a presence that was beyond any powers ever experienced. A power that is worth fighting for. My focus turned to that light. I wanted to be part of it. I couldn't sleep without praying. I woke up to pray at midnight, at 03.00 a.m. and 06.00 a.m., and then any time in the day but mostly recognised the hours 9, 12, and 3. I wanted so much to live in that light he showed me, so amongst other things, I made Psalm 91 my prayer and Psalm 16:1 my plea. 'Keep me safe O God for I have come to you for refuge.'

> I have seen violence done to the helpless and I have heard the groans of the poor. Now I will rise up to rescue them as they have longed for me to do (Ps. 12).

These are God's Words that he himself comes to the rescue. He sees every tear that falls from your eyes to the ground. Even when the enemy thinks that no one has seen their evil, God will see everything and ask your enemy about your tears. God records every action against you, every attack, every abuse, every oppression, and every wrongdoing against you. He asked Cain about Abel's whereabouts. The things that Cain thought he had done in private God punished Cain for it. He says *Vengeance is mine*; he will revenge on your behalf and when he does, you will know God has done it for you. Then you rejoice and that heals your innermost being.

Left with a dying child

Then something happened in my life that made me realise that God takes care of my needs. Cavin was working in another town, and he would come home when he was off duty. One time he came home, and our son five years old at that time had tonsillitis. The whole throat was swollen; he could not eat or drink. We took him to the doctor who recommended that he goes under operation to remove the tonsils. The problem was, we could not get him into hospital to get the operation done as all the doctors were on strike. We did not have enough money to go to a private hospital, and the medical aid we were on could not cover the costs of treatment in a private hospital. Cavin said he was going back to work. I asked if he had any money to spare so that I could try and find some help for our son, but he said he did not have. He wasn't helping me with rent, money for food, fees or clothing for the children. All the money he earned was completely for himself. He had free accommodation. Electricity and water were paid for. He had no bills at all. Transport to and from work was provided for. Where was his money going? What was he using his money for apart from giving some of it to Bev? I asked him to stay and ask for time off from work as our child was seriously ill but he said he could not. We argued, then he took off his belt and beat me up, and he went. That same night, I stayed awake praying. I could see that my son was dying. I was afraid that if I closed my eyes, when I woke up he would be gone. His body temperature was so high. I had a flannel in my hand, and I kept cooling his body to keep the temperature down. I could not take him to hospital as they were not admitting people due to doctors being on strike. God saw my desperate situation. Between 03.00 and 04.00 a.m., I drifted into sleep. This was the shortest sleep I have ever had because it lasted only a few minutes. In a dream, I saw the three angels come floating in my bedroom, and they surrounded my bed. One who was at the bottom of my bed, was fair and had the most beautiful skin I have ever seen. She was neither black nor white. She was so beautiful, and her hair was covered with a white veil like the ones Catholic sisters wear. She spoke to me in a very strong commanding voice and said, 'Pray for that child.' She threw something at me that hooked my head, and as soon as it touched me, I was ringing in tongues. Those were the most powerful tongues I had ever had from the day that I had started speaking in tongues. In that instant I was pulled up onto my knees, and I looked up towards the heavens, shouting, 'God, heal this child' over and over again. One hand was on my son and the other was raised towards heaven. As I looked up, I was starring right at the sky; there was no roof over my house. The sky was dark as if it was preparing for a heavy storm. The clouds were dark thick and dark grey. As I kept praying on top of my voice, I saw a strong flash of lighting across the sky. I woke up that instant, and I touched my son. His whole body was wet with sweat. I think my child had died or was at the point of death, and God heard my prayer and intervened. I was too young in the spirit to understand what had actually happened; all I knew was God had healed my child and I praised him. I have now grown in the spirit. I do understand that much more happened that night. My flesh was made to rest while my spirit received power and instructions to communicate with God and to ask God to heal my child. First, there was a touch of the Holy Spirit that filled me with the power of the Holy Spirit. Then I was drawn to my knees, and I started by speaking in tongues and then in the language I understand. In spirit, I was able to make the highest appeal to God. My ears of the spirit were opened to hear the instruction, then my mouth of the spirit opened, and my voice of the spirit was crying out to God, praying. My eyes of the spirit were opened to see the mysteries of the spirit world. Communication with God is more effective when you are in the spirit. It will be spirit to spirit. My child got healed that instant. When he got up at 06.00 a.m., the first thing he asked for was a cereal. The swelling to the throat was gone. He ate with no problems, and soon after that, he gathered his toys and was playing as if he had never been ill. A power had come that took away the spirit of death, sickness, my worry, my anxiety about the situation, potential depression, and my potential grief. Even though I had been physically abused the previous day, I had much to rejoice for which really comforted my heart. I had found a treasure that I was never willing to let go for the rest of my life.

A year later, God did something else for me. I had gone to pray with a friend of mine at dawn on top of a mountain. As I was praying, I went into tongues. I had a vision then; I saw the heavens open before me. I saw what looked like a man, dressed in a white robe and surrounded by a golden light descending from the heavens. Ahead of him was what looked like a white dove, also descending ahead of him.

CHAPTER 4

How *mental illness began*

> When it was time for harvest, Cain presented some of his cops
> to the lord. Abel also brought a gift, the best of his first born
> lambs from his flock. The Lord accepted Abel and his gift but
> he did not accept Cain and his gift. This made Cain very angry
> and looked dejected (Gen. 4:3).

Cain and Abel were brothers born from the first marriage of Adam and Eve. Abel was a shepherd who apparently pleased God that God did not only accept him but also accepted his offering. Cain and his offering, on the other hand, was unacceptable before God. This made Cain angry, and he looked rejected. God saw it and warned Cain about his behaviour.

Anger is nothing visible to the human eye. It is a spirit that attacks people from all walks of life. Anger opens the door to a whole lot of evil. It is the main reason behind violence and aggression, domestic violence, antisocial behaviour, rape, murder, anxiety, and self-destruction. It motivates evil, and it invites the devil to take control of one's life. Every spirit the devil imparts in a person attracts other spirits to form a chain that eventually binds the person into oppression. God saw the spirit of anger in Cain and did not approve of it. He warned Cain saying, 'Sin is crouching at the door but you must subdue it and be its master.' God knew that he had put a more powerful spirit in Cain which was able to overcome the spirit of anger and suppress it. He encouraged Cain to do what was right and to have power over the devil.

In mental illness today, anger is experienced every day, and it has destroyed so many lives. Anger has led people to be verbally and physically aggressive to others, racially abusive, perform arson attacks, murder, rape, stabbings, domestic violence, attempted murder, and many other things. Anger is treated using medication, counselling, and therapies, such as anger management and cognitive behaviour therapy. All these are aimed at dealing with anger and being able to suppress it. This is not enough; the person being treated needs to have the will power within themselves to be able to suppress their anger. If this is not there, then therapies and medication will only offer short-term results. This power from within is essential to treatment. In Christians, we believe this power comes from the Holy Spirit and from Jesus Christ who resides in us. Nothing can drive out or attack the spirit of anger except the spirit of God himself.

Having been rejected by God and his offering, having been unacceptable to God, Cain was filled with jealousy over his brother. Even though God had warned him, he did not listen as he was already preoccupied with thoughts of killing. Jealousy is also identified as a symptom of mental illness. People who are jealous do not want to see good things happening to others. It leads them into all sorts of feelings and emotions. Like Cain, they start having wicked thoughts about those people they are jealous of. They become paranoid, make all sorts of accusations about them, and they would do anything to jeopardise other people's happiness. Cain decided to get rid of his brother but that created more problems for him as it invited the curse of the Lord upon his life. When God asked Cain where his brother was, Cain lied.

God was not happy with Cain and he cursed him. Cain had acted against God and other people. He was banished from the land, was made homeless and a wanderer. The presence of God departed from him, exposing him to the devil. He was now without God's protection. His life was now surrounded by darkness and the door for the devil to enter was now open. These curses were from God himself, and there was no one who could take them away from Cain, for it is written, the word of the Lord is sent it out and it always produces fruit, and it accomplishes whatever God wants it to accomplish. (Isa. 55:11) At that time, there was no one to redeem the human race from the curses made upon them by God, for it is only God who can take the curse away. This curse was taken away by Jesus, and today, it no longer exists in people who believe in Jesus Christ. The word of the Lord says he who hung on the tree took the curse away. The devil saw this happen to Cain and has held on to those spirits and is now using them to attack whenever he gets a chance.

Cain was afraid that if discovered by his relatives, he would be killed for revenge. A spirit of worry and fear (phobia) was born in him. Notice that this spirit came in when God's presence had left. Fear of being killed by his relatives. Cain was not afraid before but when God warned him about the devil, he did not pay attention to it. The devil then drove this spirit into him amongst other spirits. It is not a good spirit. That is why God had warned Cain, knowing that the devil was going to fill him with the spirits of jealousy and murder. After this, Cain was filled with fear. The spirit of fear is quite prevalent in people with mental illness today to the point that some become dysfunctional. Phobias now are called by different names. Cain became isolated from his family and friends. The devil put him in a corner where he began to torment him. Isolation, worry, and loneliness often lead to depression. The person has no social life. In times of trouble, they have no one to turn to and this can be distressful. However, despite Cain's sin, God promised that if anyone attacked Cain, then that person would be punished seven times more. Lemech, a great-great-great-grandson of Cain, also committed murder in self-defence. What Cain had done became a generational curse, and people continued to sin until God decided to wipe them out with floods of water.

God also cursed Cain with the spirit of fruitless labour, for he said he was going to harvest very little from the land even if he worked hard. In other words, this was an introduction to Cain of the spirit of poverty. In the world today, anyone who commits murder is locked up and becomes unproductive, or they are locked up with hard labour.

Symptoms of mental illness from Cain's case

> Paranoia—Cain was paranoid that his relatives might kill
> him
> Violence and aggression
> jealousy
> feelings of being rejected
> causing harm to others
> killing
> homicidal thoughts
> Phobia
> Isolation
> Anger

Curses Cain received from God: These are still issues that arise with people suffering mental illness

> Homelessness
> Poverty
> fruitlessness—vulnerability to exploitation. Being used by
> other people.

Although the Bible does not give a full account of his life when he was living on his own, there is a possibility that he suffered a lot of issues, such as mental torture because he had killed his brother, loneliness as he was away from his loved ones, anxiety, confusion, stress over thoughts of being on his own and of killing, hunger, guilt, and starvation as God had told him he was not going to get enough from the soil, flashbacks of the incident of killing, and in all mental distress. All these spirits had room in him.

Spirit of depression

When Saul was commanded by God to completely destroy the Amalekites nation and all their belongings, he disobeyed God. (1 Sam. 15:3) Saul captured the Amalekite king and spared his life and kept the best sheep, goats, cattle, fat cattle, and fat calves. God rejected Saul and God's presence left Saul.

Now the spirit of the lord had left Saul and the lord sent him a tormenting spirit that filled him with depression and fear.

For the spirit of fear and depression to enter Saul, God's presence had left, for Cain to be attacked by evil spirits, God's presence had left. Without the presence of the Holy Spirit in us, we become susceptible to attacks by the devil. The spirits of depression, anger, jealousy, loneliness, fear, homelessness, poverty, and many other unwanted spirits are not from God. They are evil spirits because they cause human life to be miserable. They are not visible to the human eye but their effects are devastating and can be felt and seen manifesting in the physical world. The evil behaviour comes out of a person because these evil spirits are residing in them. In mental health today, it is mostly the seen behaviour that determines the diagnosis. We hear that Saul tried to kill David during one of his attacks by the spirits. The spirit of murder was the driving force. One might argue that but it was God who drove these spirits into them, how can they be evil? It shows that God has authority over all these spirits; however, what God has done no man can undo. God did this in his anger. It needed God himself to drive the spirit out of Saul, no one else could. But God has forgiven us now. This is why Jesus came to redeem us from these curses and these spirits. Today, we are lucky because we have got a redeemer who has the power to redeem us from any illness. Every single one of the demons was taken to the cross, and in our lives today, if we believe in Jesus Christ, we know we will be saved from mental illness. The devil knowing the distress mental illness causes in people is now using this spirit to torment people. Jesus came and wiped all the curses, but why is the world still suffering from these spirits?

The devil fights hard to make sure that people lack knowledge of the power of the presence of God in them. He causes people to hate Jesus Christ, not read the Bible, and sin against God. This way he knows there would be room for him to enter, torment, and manipulate people. The word says, 'He is roaming the earth seeking who to devour.' Most people suffer depression today and go through psychiatric treatments. All treatments are aimed at lifting their mood. Other people will self-medicate and end up taking drugs and alcohol. All this does not take the depression away. The word says, 'The joy of the Lord is my strength.' It is that joy and peace that the Holy Spirit brings into us which uplifts and strengthens us. It is the natural joy of the Lord. God's spirit brings a calming effect within a person. It brings peace and joy. Any tormenting spirit is not of God but God has power and authority over all spirits. The presence of God has Jesus, the Holy Spirit, and God himself, and it drives the spirits out.

Some of the things you see in a person suffering from a depressive attack.

The spirit of depression follows a certain pattern in all those it attacks:

> Low mood—some people call this low spirits
> Irritability—tendency to respond with undue annoyance to minor demands
> Lack of interest and enjoyment—even in the things they used to like
> Sleep disturbance
> Pessimistic thoughts—only sees the unhappy side of things
> Agitation—restlessness due to being unable to relax
> Suicidal thoughts
> Lack of confidence
> Isolating oneself
> Feelings of hopelessness
> Lack of appetite
> Sleep disturbance
> Low self-esteem
> Self-harm to ease the pain

This attack on the spirit can have some crippling effects. It can cause people to lose their jobs, become homeless, destabilise families and marriages, and many other things. In my work, I have come across people who suffer depression, and it is triggered by various things, such as loss of a job, a relative, a house, mounting bills, divorce, and other unpleasant events.

CHAPTER 5

Domestic Violence and Mental Illness

Spirit of fear

Domestic violence is not acceptable before God. Anger is displayed, and this opens the door to evil. The perpetrator of violence is afraid of being discovered and be dealt with according to the law. The recipients of violence often keep quiet because they are threatened that if they tell, then worse things will happen to them. The spirit of fear is often reflected in anxiety and panic attacks. In mental health today it is termed as phobia. It manifests itself in many different ways. Some people become afraid of accessing areas where the violence took place for fear of meeting their abusers. Others cannot even access shops because of fear of meeting their abusers. In the worst cases, some victims cannot even get outside their homes. 'God has not given us a spirit of fear. He has given unto us a spirit of love. A spirit of power and a sound mind'. It is quite clear that fear is not of the Lord. When it becomes intense, people often suffer panic attacks and anxiety. People get admitted in mental health hospitals for treatment but it is very hard for them to recover completely.

Schizophrenia

Schizophrenia is one form of mental illness that has demonstrated to me that there is a world of spirits. The spirit of schizophrenia makes contact with the outside world. When it resides in a person, the person starts to get out of this world experiences. It makes the person talk to the unseen, visualise, taste, and smell things from the spiritual world. The person responds by talking back to the voices or doing what the voice is telling them to do. I have heard people with schizophrenia saying, 'The voice is telling me to hit or kill people.' Sometimes they hear voices and recognise them as voices of the people/person who abused them in the past. Others would recognise the voice and would say it is a male or female voice. A lady once reported seeing skeletons ripping her flesh off. The experiences can be very terrifying. In the Bible, prophets of God reported seeing visions and hearing God's voice but no one has ever been reported to have been tormented or to have lost their mind. The devil uses the same mechanisms but his ways are different in that they are tormenting to the human being. People would hear things and visualise things but unlike prophets, their experiences are tormenting. Due to schizophrenia, some people have suffered domestic violence due to the voices voices telling the Abuser to hit or kill their partners.

Paranoia

So much paranoia is expressed in domestic violence. The abuser is paranoid of the victim's behaviour as they have fear of being reported or of the victim escaping. On the other hand, the victim is also paranoid of every action the abuser takes. They are wary of that hand when it is lifted up; they do not know where it will land. They are wary of any movement the abuser makes as they do not know when next it is targeted at them. The Abuser is paranoid of what the victim says and can easily turn things said in good faith into something unpleasant.

Suicide and self-harm

Some women become hopeless and see no future at all. The pain is so great that they cannot handle it. Some have killed themselves by slashing their veins and bleeding to death, others have hung themselves, and others have not succeeded, and after a failed attempt, they have ended up in psychiatric hospital. Some women still carry the thoughts of suicide and will try by all means to discretely plan it and carry it through although many times without success. Others will self-harm by cutting themselves with sharp objects on their arms to release pain. All the same, all this is a call for help. They need help to get out of their sufferings. I could be any of them.

Domestic violence makes the victim feel helpless, hopeless, abused, hurt, angry, and ashamed. Sometimes the victim is intimidated and cannot tell people of what is happening to them for fear of worse things happening to them. Some women are starved if the man is the breadwinner; they are threatened with losing their homes, children and they see themselves as homeless.

Alcoholism and substance misuse

Some women will turn to drinking heavily and others to using drugs as a way of coping with what they are going through. This can have detrimental effects to their health.

Working with women who have suffered or are suffering mental health, you find that some women either they cannot trust anyone and they do not want to talk about it or they have no one to talk to. They have nowhere to pre-empty their thoughts and feelings. Their anxieties and fears grow. The pain, hurt, and feelings remain bottled up in them. They are like someone in a deep dark hole, and they see no way out. In my case, what helped me most was praying because during prayer, I felt that someone was listening and there was someone who was giving me comfort, someone who never criticised me or say go away or say make an appointment or say I can't speak to you now I'm busy. It was my belief. I was able to trust God and believed he was there for me, and the more I read the Bible the more reassurance I got from the words I read.

I have seen women who have had mental breakdown due to domestic violence, some of them suffer from posttraumatic stress disorder (PTSD), some people call it 'flashbacks' due to horrific things that have happened to them. Some have ended up with severe depression. The worst case I saw was of a woman who refused to talk. She did not say a word for days even when the children visited. She just sat there, looking down, never making eye contact, and anyone who did not know her would think she was dumb. Other women related stories of losing the babies they were carrying due to physical aggression towards them. Some suffered from panic attacks; they panic over very little things but because that fear which was instilled in them has crippled their lives, they cannot control their fear. Others won't even go out to do shopping due to fear of meeting their abusers. Some have even suffered worse mental health problems.

The spirit of domestic violence also transfers itself from the abuser to the victim. Some victims after being abused become so bitter, so angry, so hurt, and cannot control themselves. The victim will seek revenge and in so doing, hit back at the abuser using dangerous weapons. Some have used hot irons, boiling water, or hot oil. Others have used knives to stab their abusers, and others have even shot at their abusers. These victims have ended up being tried under the law and have ended up being locked up in jail and then transferred to mental health hospital for treatment. It is sad that these victims have lost their children, their homes, and their lives because of the anger that was wrongly channelled. They were once quite normal people, leading a normal life but now they are mental health victims. The Lord showed me all these things to show how he saved me. It was talking to him that helped me and led me out of the path of retaliation. I could be any of these victims. Nothing could have stopped me from stabbing Cavin' or hitting him with a metal bar on his head. It is the guidance of the Holy Spirit that led me from that path. Like all these women, there is nothing that could have stopped me from having flashbacks of all the abuse and even the strangulation that I experienced. Somehow, a blanket came and overshadowed my thoughts that these strong memories were quickly erased from my mind. I wanted to know more about this mental illness. How come someone who was leading a normal life would suddenly be termed mentally ill after engaging in an act of revenge by murdering or causing bodily harm to the abuser. Why would all of sudden someone be labelled mentally ill after causing injury or death during domestic violence? Why the sudden jump from being in one state of the mind to another? How does this happen? During my journey of reading the Bible as instructed in my dream, I was surprised to see that even in the Bible there are records of violence leading to mental illness. The story of Cain and Abel is the first. Cain's life drastically changed soon after murdering Abel. These victims labelled with mental illness end up exhibiting violent behaviours and other behaviours associated with mental illness. The story of Saul is one of disobedience; this also led to mental illness.

CHAPTER 6

Jesus and the demons of mental illness

When Jesus arrived at the other side of the lake in the region of the Gadarenes, two men, who were possessed by demons, came to meet him. They lived in the cemetery, and they were so violent that no one could go through the area. Matthew 8:28

Matthew mentions two men. During that time, these men were regarded as unclean because they were gentiles, they lived in the cemetery, and they were demon possessed. Jesus had crossed over to a region of the gentiles. These were people who were regarded as unworthy of the kingdom of God. These men despite being gentiles, they were controlled by evil spirits and had left them violent, isolated from everyone, living among the dead, and threatening to the whole community. The question is, how did these men survive, what did they eat, and for how long had they lived like this?

> So they arrived in the region of the Gadarenes across the lake of Galilee. As Jesus was climbing out of the boat, a man possessed by demons came to meet him. For a long time he had been homeless and naked, living in a cemetery outside the town (Luke 8:26).

Luke picks out the issue of homelessness and nakedness and living among the dead. A cemetery is not a place for the living; it is a place for the dead. The spirits that were controlling this person's life could not stand living among the people in the land of the living; they wanted to live among the dead. They chose the place for the dead, and they were comfortable living there. There was a connection between the spirits living in this man with the spirits of the dead. Obviously, these were wondering or tormented spirits of the dead that did not make it to heaven. Those that had gone to heaven were surely in a beautiful place which they could not give it up to live in a cemetery. During the transfiguration, we hear that the disciples saw Moses and Elijah. It could never be spirits of such people found living in the cemetery. These were unclean spirits.

Luke also mentions that the man was homeless and naked. Homelessness is curse that we first saw God giving to Cain. If God made the first clothes and covered Adam and Eve, why would then would God leave someone running around naked. This clearly shows that this is not the work of God but of the devil. He always works against God and tries every time to discredit God's work. Luke goes on to say that this man had been put under guard and put in chains and shackles; he still broke them and ran out into the wilderness, completely under the demon's power. The power that the possessed man had was too much for any human being to handle. They tried using other mechanisms of tying him up in chains but still he overpowered the chains. Nothing could restrain him. I have seen this in my work. The strength that a mentally ill person has when they become violent is overwhelming. A very young girl, about ten stone in weight would take ten strong men to restrain. Then one would ask where all this power is coming from. It is occult and invisible to the human eye. A group of demons has more strength than a normal human being. Fighting it in the flesh is not easy; the demons are too powerful. Many people, therefore, do not want to pray for demon-possessed individuals for fear of being beaten up.

Mark gives an account of the same event, and he says that the man was possessed by an evil spirit, and he came out from a cemetery to meet Jesus. Mark also says *this man lived among burial caves and was no longer restrained, even with chains.* This shows how powerful demonic activity can be. *Day and night the man wandered among the burial caves and the hills howling and cutting himself with sharp stones.* (Mark 5:4-5) The man was restless; he could not sleep, and he was self-harming.

If this man was to be brought to hospital today, his mental health assessment would have included the following:

Homelessness

Isolation

Violence/aggression

Wandering the cemetery/burial caves, and hills

Self-harming by cutting self with sharp stones

Insomnia

Poor diet

Self neglect

Stripping in public

Unkempt

Running away/absconsion risk

Danger to public

The man would have been detained in hospital for treatment. A restraint team would have been set up to manage him in times of aggression and violence. His dietary needs would have been catered for, personal hygiene attended to, given clothing, medication, accommodation, and have all his basic needs taken care of. However, this could have not taken the mental illness away. The medication could help the physical body to rest and relax but the mental illness would be there. Today in mental health, this is very common. People have tried to run away when they are detained, others strip in public areas, and there is a lot of violence and aggression. Doors are broken; windows, chairs, and knives are used to threaten or harm others. In most cases, the urge to self-harm or to kill manifests itself. It is usually taken seriously when threats to harm or kill someone are expressed because they can be so unpredictable that nothing is taken for granted with them. The sense of dignity is sometimes lost, and all they want to do is stay naked. Some spend the night awake, shouting, screaming, banging walls and doors. Domestic violence can also lead to all this.

Mark 5:6 says, *The man ran to meet Jesus and bowed low before him with a shriek and screamed.* Jesus asked for the name of the spirit and it answered *legion, for we are many'* (*Legion means the largest unit of a roman army consisting of 3,000-6,000 men*).

This explains why the man was so powerful, why he terrorised the whole area where he was staying, why he broke chains, and why no one could challenge him. His presentation shows us some of the spirits that possessed him, such as the spirit of nakedness, isolation, poverty, living among the dead, wandering, violence, homelessness, and many more. In mental illness, there is always more than one spirit possessing a person. The spirits are seen through the behaviours that are observed, however, some spirits would be hiding and these are often difficult to detect. This explains why sometimes it is difficult to come up with a diagnosis as it is hard to say exactly what is observed. Every category of similar presentation has a common name that embraces the behaviours, for example, schizophrenia, depression, stress, and many more. Some of the behaviours may not fit into any of the categories and may be very difficult to manage. These just end up being termed challenging behaviours. But as revealed to us by Jesus Christ, these demonic spirits can exist in one person in large numbers and they have names. However, all of them bowed to Jesus. Mark says, *With a shriek, they screamed, why are you interfering with me, Jesus, son of the most high.* The whole army of the devil, 3,000-6,000 demons, was bowing down worshipping Jesus. Isn't that amazing? There were no chains used to physically bind the demons but they were bound in the spirit. They were even told what to do. Demons listened to the instructions given by Jesus. The man calmed down and showed no violence at all. With Jesus in us, violence is controlled.

How did Jesus conquer the evil spirit?

The word of the Lord says, in Genesis 1:2 'In the beginning the spirit of the lord was hovering over the water.' From there God created the world through his word. Now Jesus had come to reestablish the kingdom of God, not only in human beings but also in all creation. When Jesus said to his disciples, let us cross over to the other side, he had seen a whole territory that needed redemption: the trees, hills, the waters, and even man. As he was going over the water, he was re-establishing the kingdom of God over the waters. The demons in the region saw him coming, and they set out to fight him. They wanted to drown him and his disciples, but when he spoke, they all calmed. The water obeyed. This was the voice of creation, powerful, and mighty. The water recognised it, the wind recognised it, and even the land and the hills beyond. The whole atmosphere acknowledged his presence. Suddenly, the control that the devil had over the territory was lost. The waters, the hills, the caves, the graves, and the land of the Gadarenes was liberated and redeemed from the hold of the devil. The demons in the man lost control of the man, because the flesh recognised its creator and was delivered to its original state. The demons that had been using the body could not use that body any more. They were subdued by the body. The spirit of the Lord had taken control, and the devil lost all control. The mountains in their joy, the hills, the caves, the graves, and the flesh that had housed the demons all responded to the voice of creation. The demons had nowhere to run but had to surrender to Jesus. They even begged with Jesus to decide a better fate for them. Where was the devil, their ruler? They bowed at Jesus' feet, worshipped, and begged him not to send them to the pit of fire. Demons are fallen angels who joined with Satan in his rebellion with God. So if demons are fallen angels, then they were once inhabitants of the heavens. They are spirits and they are evil. They know God, the Holy Spirit and certainly Jesus. They have names like any other angel in the heavenly realms as we hear about Michael or Gabriel. This is the reason Jesus asked for a name. When he said, legion, this indicated a large number of evil spirits that had come to live in the man. This explains the strength of the unseen forces that had come to possess the man, and any ordinary man could not come against. This was an army that was raging war against mankind, and this was the reason why they had terrorised the whole area. What people saw was a man they knew breaking chains, violent, terrorising the whole area, and cutting himself with sharp stones. A man who had lost his family, friends, and with no social network. What was unseen was this whole army of demons. These demons are spirits and cannot be fought in the flesh but in the spirit. Jesus being the son of God, filled with the spirit of God, was able to see and recognise them. He had no mercy with them; they were and are still his enemy. Every time we hear that he cast out the evil spirit and people received their miracle. This was his mission to redeem the children of God from the evil works of the devil. This is the role of the church today, but the church must be anchoring on the foundations of God the Father, Jesus the Son, and the Holy Spirit. The movement of the Holy Spirit must be in full control. Demons will then just fall at their feet and worship Jesus. As children of God, the church should be able to exercise its authority over the demons, cast them out, and send them off to the pit of fire and in doing so, liberate the children of God. If Jesus did it and then send the children of God to do the same, then this should be the mission of the church besides preaching the word. By casting out demons, people get healed and get delivered from painful and difficult situations. A church that does not have the movement of the Holy Spirit is dead, as it will be operating in the flesh, and the flesh cannot fight things of the spirit.

For we are not fighting against flesh and blood enemies, but against rulers and authorities of the unseen world, against mighty powers in the dark world, and against evil spirits in the heavenly places. (Eph. 6:12).

The kingdom of God is spiritual and so is the kingdom of the devil. You join the kingdom of God, you automatically fight the opposition to win battles for God. You are a soldier for God, and you need your weapons strong and mighty. The fight is in the spirit. The only way to win is when you are in the spirit. Flesh against spirit will never work. That is why the devil targets the mind so that you remain suppressed under his powers. There are churches today which do not allow people to speak in tongues. Communication with God is in the spirit and speaking in tongues is the key to a direct communication with God. (Rom. 8:26-28)

Jesus did something then; he cast the demons out and send them into the pigs. This shows how he can command even the armies of the devil without any opposition. The demons in their thousands obeyed him and went into the pigs. Now Jesus had re-established his authority over the waters when he told the waters to calm on his way to the reigion. The pigs drowned, and the demons were left without a body to live in. Emmanuel Eni in his article *Delivered from the Powers of Darkness* states that he was an agent of the devil and that the devil has a beautiful city build under the sea where he holds meetings with his agents and does most of his activities there. This is under the waters, not over the waters. As the spirit of God hovers over the waters, the devil is suppressed underneath.

CHAPTER 7

How the works of my fathers and my ancestors attracted demons

God had helped me to forget and heal in so many ways but forgiving Cavin and his sister for what they had done to me was very difficult. I struggled with it for a long time. It was like a worm eating me from within. I carried a bitterness within me that no one could cure until one day Cavin had gone to make more plans with his sister Bev that were going to affect the whole family tremendously. As the two elderly children had grown and left home, the whole burden of looking after our younger son was again left for me. I had thought he was going to help save university fees for our son. This was not going to happen. It meant again I was going to continue to struggle on my own. I had raised up my daughter to university, paying for everything. It pained me so much. This was a married man going out of his home all the time to make plans about life with his sister. He was not committed to our marriage at all. I needed no one to tell me Cavin did not care about us. I made a decision on that day to move forward and start my life afresh. I needed a new beginning. It was very painful to think that this still happened even after twenty-one years of marriage.

At that moment, there was a pastor ministering on TV. A word came to my heart to ring him for prayer. I just felt the love of God so overwhelming that I started to cry silently. At first, I could not get through as the lines were busy. I took his number, and I rang him immediately after the programme. I just said to him, 'Please pray for me, I want a new beginning.' I said this in a calm voice.

He asked me if I had children and if I was married. Then he surprised me by saying, 'Stop crying.' I had not done anything to give away my crying and then he said, 'People have let you down in the past. I am going to pray that you forgive them.' I had not told him anything about my life or my problems. A new beginning can be a new beginning from drugs, alcohol, or prostitution. How did he know that I had disappointments from my past and how did he know that I needed to forgive some people. He prayed for the spirit of forgiveness to fill me. God heals in his own time but the healing process was going to be painful and revealing on all things that concern my life from birth.

Demons are angels of the devil but originally were created in the heavens. They once were servants of the most high God, running errands for him. They have knowledge of the heavens and of God's children. They rebelled against God, and they were thrown out of the heavens together with their leader, the devil. They act contrary to God's will. Their plans are evil, and they lead man to despise God in the hope of recruiting many into their kingdom. Their actions are crippling to the soul, the spirit, and the flesh. They leave behind them some very undesirable and devastating effects. God revealed me the altars that my fathers and my great-great-great ancestors had build. The altars that still had a hold on my life. Some of them still operational today. God wanted me to know how as a family, as a village, as a town, and as a nation we had offended him through our actions. The altars that my ancestors had built had to be pulled down. The foundations that had been built for my life fell short of everything God desired; as a result I entered a cursed marriage.

Exposed to Demons at birth

The Lord began to show me things that I needed to understand. I was born and grew up in a culture and tradition that believed in the powers of spirit mediums, witch doctors, and spirits of the dead. When a woman was pregnant, she was taken to a witch doctor or a spirit medium and given some medicines to help her have a safe delivery. This is against God's Word.

> ... and do not let people practice fortune-telling, or use sorcery, or interpret omens or engage in witchcraft or cast spells or function as mediums, or psychics or call the spirits of the dead (Deut. 18:10-11).

This was completely against God as the witch doctors cast spells. Sometimes women were told that they were going to have a difficult delivery. They were given some concussions to burn and were told these were for sending evil spirits away or were given some mixtures to drink or have some incisions done to their skin using a razor blade. Powder was then rubbed into the cuttings on their skins. Emmanuel Eni in his document (*Delivered from the Powers of Darkness* on www.spiritlessons. com) explains that witch doctors are agents of the devil and they go into the underworld and get ashes of dead people from the devil. They rub these into the cuttings they make on people's skins. No one had any idea what was happening. They believed in it and saw no harm in doing it. Whatever the mother eats affects the unborn child. The same blood that flows in the mother's body is the same blood that flows in the unborn child. The medicines and the concussions they took also affected the unborn child. The blood covenant in which the mother engaged was going to affect the life and the destiny of the child. It is at this point that the devil takes control of the child's destiny before the child is even born. This is how children's destinies were reversed before they were born. The moment the mother engages in these rituals, the presence of God leaves and the child is born into a world where he or she is controlled by the devil. When Hannah got pregnant, it was through prayer. The pregnancy of Mary was from God. In the spiritual world of the kingdom of God pregnancies are known and children are assigned to different people for different purposes in the world. Children are given by God. However, because of our actions, the actions our parents, grandparents, ancestors, and which are sometimes contrary to God's commandments, the doors are opened for the devil to control our lives. Then problems arise, children turn out to be what you never wanted them to be, murderers, prostitutes, robbers, alcohol addicts, rapists, and other negative behaviours. Parents often blame the circle of friends the children get involved with but what is it that draws these children to these circles of friends. God said in Isaiah 54 *I will teach your children* but once you have abandoned God, then the devil gets his way with your children.

I do not know what happened on Cavin's side, and I have no idea what my mother ate while I was in the womb. I don't know what covenants she entered into or what my grandparents did. But God showed me how the devil easily captures the unborn into his circle. The roots of the child's destiny unknowingly become planted in the devil's kingdom that no matter how you try to nurture or teach the child. The devil remains in control. In our culture and tradition, there was disobedience to God through ignorance but nevertheless, God regards it as disobedience and Deuteronomy 28:20 says about disobedience: *The Lord himself will send on you curses, confusion and frustration in everything you do, until you are at last completely destroyed for doing evil and abandoning him.* The child therefore is already cursed before it is born. The life ahead is full of frustration and confusion, which will ultimately cause mental distress. This is one of the traps that the devil uses to control people's lives. What did your parents get involved in when your mother was pregnant with you? What vows did they make? What foods and medicines were given to your mother to eat during rituals and feasts? Was it food offered to idols? Did she eat any foods offered to other gods? Did she enter any blood covenants? It is a blessing today that we have Jesus who died on the cross to take all our sins away. When a woman was in the eighth month of her pregnancy, she was taken back to her parents to give birth. On the day she went to her parents' house, a goat was killed and a piece of meat was roasted. This piece of meat was offered to the ancestors and then it was tradition that it should be eaten without salt. Therefore, as this tradition was done by almost everyone, how many children escaped the hands of the devil?

When a child was born, he or she had to be taken back to the witch doctors to be given more medicines to protect the child, and one that was plastered on the baby spot meant to help the skull to grow and close up. The question is, what mixtures were those? Did the mixture also contain dead people's ashes? One can never tell what it was. The Lord showed me that this was a way in which the devil made strong connections with the child. Then later in life things start to happen, and you do not understand what has gone wrong, but there is that unseen spirit holding the reigns of your life and your children's lives. That same spirit that held your ancestors' lives.

Life led by demons

In my culture it was a tradition to consult spirit mediums and witch doctors on issues concerning life. The dead were believed in, so much that up to this day this is still happening. One year after a person had died, a spirit medium or a witch doctor was consulted to guide people in the ceremony to bring the spirit of the dead person back to the family. It was a belief that the dead would be protecting the family and guiding them into prosperity. The witch doctors or the spirit mediums guided the family on what to buy and how to perform the ceremony. Families were given concussions to use for bathing, and these were meant to drive the evil spirits away. They were also given some herbs to burn and let the smoke cover their bodies while they also inhaled some of the smoke. This was done before the ceremony. This tradition happened for generations and to think that if all the dead spirits were brought back for all these generations, what effects do they had on the living. If they were cursed when they were still alive, wasn't this a way of bringing the curses back to the family? This ceremony was done for every dead person. It did not matter if they were a good person or a bad person. God promises to prosper those who obey his commands and call unto his name. The devil was also claiming that by doing this, people would prosper. That is how the devil deceives people. This was a tradition that opened the door to evil. God says you shall have no other God besides me and yet people were inviting the dead to look after them instead of inviting God to look after them.

Every family had one big ancestral spirit that they believed looked after them. This was said to be a spirit of a great-great-grandfather from generations back. This spirit would manifest on one member of the family and would instruct people on how to perform ceremonies and rituals. The spirit would instruct people on what was needed for offering as sacrifice and how the ceremony was to be conducted. The spirit would say if there was going to be rain or drought, what caused droughts and what needed to be done to appease the spirits of the angry forefathers. The process of the manifestation of this ancestral spirit followed a similar pattern to all families. One member of the family would suddenly get critically ill. A witch doctor or spirit medium was usually consulted to tell what was wrong with the person and to get treatment. The witch doctor or spirit medium would say it was a spirit of a great-great-grandfather that wanted to manifest on the person. The family was instructed to buy cloth, swords, a staff, wooden plate, snuff, and a cow that would be used as sacrifice. They were instructed to brew beer and prepare a cow for offering. The beer took seven days to brew. First the grain had to be offered to the spirits and then the grain was soaked before it was brewed. The ceremony was done overnight; the whole family was invited. All distant relatives would come to see if the spirit manifested and hear what the spirit had to say. During the night, there was singing, dancing, and drums played throughout the night.

I saw demons talk, drink, and dance

It was usually in the middle of the night that the spirit manifested. The spirit would start by howling and growling like a lion. Meanwhile everyone would be clapping hands, welcoming the spirit. When the spirit spoke, the first thing it said was, 'I am very tired. I have come from very far can I have some water?' Reading Bill Wiese's '23 *Minutes in Hell* 'on Spirit Lessons on the Internet, Bill explains about the fires in hell and how the spirits there were desperate for water. I was shocked when I realised that the spirits people were evoking, believing in, offering sacrifices to, and putting their full trust in to lead and guide them were actually spirits from hell. Why would any spirit come claiming to be so thirsty and demanding water immediately before anything else and of all things why water? This was an awakening call for me. For generations, my ancestors were dealing in demonic ceremonies. Offering food and sacrifices to demons of hell. This explained to me why I had suffered all this domestic violence, fruitless labour, frustrations, and stress. The disobedience for God had been carried on for generations by my ancestors. In Hosea 4:6, the Lord says, 'My people perish because of lack of knowledge.' Here were thousands of families calling out for help from spirits from hell, condemned spirits. How was God going to be happy with this nation? They had no idea what they were doing to themselves and to their children. They were evoking spirits of hell, spirits of murder, prostitution, blasphemy against God, poverty, paedophilic, thieving, and many more. These were purely demonic spirits that people worshipped, respected, and trusted in.

The manifested spirit would introduce itself after drinking water and usually, it would say the name of an ancestor long gone. In most cases who no one had ever seen but only heard of. The possessed person would use the walking stick bought to walk like an old person and would talk like an old person in a language from generations back. That poorly and near-to-death person becomes strong again and would dance with so much strength. The person possessed by the demon spirit would then drink blood from a bull. If they did this successfully, then people would say this was a genuine spirit. Once the spirit was accepted in the family, it started telling people about their future. In Leviticus 17:10-14, the word of the Lord warns people about eating or drinking blood in any form, that they will be cut off from the community. The word says in verse 14,

You must never eat or drink blood, for the life of any creature is in its blood. So whoever consumes blood should be cut off from the community.

When Christians take holy communion and drink wine as a symbol of the blood of Jesus, the actual blood of Jesus is spiritual that is why it is available for everyone who calls on his name all over the world. The blood of Jesus gives the life of Jesus to the believers so that the believers are empowered to live the life of Christ. By drinking blood from animals, one would be hoping to get the life of an animal in them. How could someone created by God as a human being, ever want the life of an animal in them. Would this please God? This was purely an act of disobedience to God which had serious implications like those Cain experienced. To be made homeless, a wanderer because one has been cut off from the community. This was a curse. My ancestors in these rituals they performed consumed blood. They were cursed and this made sense to me. The spirit still followed me. I had worked and invested in a house that was stolen from me. This aim of the curse upon my forefathers was to make me homeless. This was a generational curse.

The possessed person would drink the brewed beer; a cupful was poured to the ground, and this was meant to be for all the other dead relatives. The possessed person would demand what food he wanted to eat, usually the person would refuse to eat food with spices or onion. The person did not like perfume or scented soaps, and anyone smelling of perfume would be sent away from the ceremony. It was all strange. The affected person began to behave in strange ways, such as smoking snuff and sometimes eating it. But I have learnt that demons eat, talk, walk, see, have knowledge about people's lives, jobs, and families. Why using a staff? The devil would copy everything that God did and what is recorded in the Bible. Moses had a staff when he led the people of Israel out of captivity and so the spirit mediums had staffs as well and demanded that one be bought for them if there wasn't one. Ezekiel in his book Chapter 2: verses 1-9 describes his experiences with God and says, he heard a voice speaking to him and the voice said to him, 'Son of man, I want to speak with you' He says, 'The spirit came into me, as he spoke and he set me on my feet.' The devil follows the same pattern of getting into people and using them the way he wants to. God's prophets tell about the future and give messages about God. Ezekiel carries on to say, 'The voice said to him, "Son of man eat what I am giving you-eat the scroll".' The devil and his demons do the same. They make the people in whom they have taken residence eat the food they demand for sacrifice. People also ate food offered to idols through demands made by witch doctors. They were told to kill certain animals and cook them in certain ways and eat them. The doors for the devil to control people's lives were made wide open by the offerings and celebrations which were against God. No wonder why most people's lives never got better but remained tormented.

In cases where all the sacrifices and offerings were done, the demon stayed comfortable because they were made welcome and were accepted. Where a demon was rejected, there was often devastating effects. I had a relative who became very ill. A witch doctor was consulted but when the spirit that was tormenting her manifested, most people in the family rejected it saying that the dead person used to be a witch. People did not respond to its demands. The person possessed by the spirit turned violent, accusing people of trying to kill her, howling, screaming, and shouting abuses. This is the same spirit that had manifested, claiming to be one of a dead relatives but could not stand rejection. When it was rejected, the spirit became very cold and calculating. The person was admitted in the hospital and diagnosed with mental illness. She claimed that there were many of them and started naming other dead relatives, saying they were also present. This same thing happens today; when Christians recognise demons and reject them or try to cast them out, they are often met with a very strong resistance and sometimes violence. It is why most Christian chose not to cast out demons because they are afraid of being physically attacked. They would rather choose to run churches where demons can come in and be comfortable and walk out without any opposition. But is that why Jesus came? Did he come to nurse demons? No, of course not; Jesus was and is still no friend to demons. He cast them out without thinking twice.

CHAPTER 8

The Bound Spirit

Why did Jesus come to save us? Growing up as a Christian and being a Christian for many years, I did not understand what it means to be free. I did not understand what it meant to be delivered or why I need Jesus, God the Father and The Holy Spirit in me, when I read the Bible, I just looked at everything as stories from the past, in other words history. I was bound, still going to church but bound. When I married, I switched from Catholic church to Cavin's church. It took me years to know that the Word of God was real, it's active and it's true. In the church, there were so many rules that even when I started praying in tongues, I had to do it outside the church because in tongues were not allowed in our church. I was ignorant of what the Word of the Lord was telling me until one day after reading the Bible, I began to pray in tongues. A new thing was revealed to me, as I started to switch from tongues to my language; I realised I was interpreting and explaining what I had read. When I spoke in my language, I was explaining what I had read. I carried on doing this and after prayer, I realised I had gained a deeper understanding of the word. The Lord told me it was the revelation spirit that had come to reveal the word to me and that the Word of God is life. As surely as God lives, the word is alive. I was given a new understanding and respect of the word. This is only possible with the spirit of the Lord present in you. Why didn't this happen to me in all the years I had been a Christian. I was a bound spirit in a church. All the curses that my ancestors and my father had acquired through their disobedience to God were still binding me. I needed to be born again. I did not understand what it meant to have a personal relationship with Jesus. This explains my years of abuse. Although I knew Jesus, I still did not know how to use the weapons of war. The devil still had a hold on me due to this ignorance and the unforgiving spirit which was in me.

When I was born, my father and his family worshipped other gods. My mother did not approve of my father's beliefs. Although she went to church, at that time she was carrying me both my grandmothers believed in the traditional consultations and rituals for safe delivery. This was against God. The influence of the family and tradition was so great that my mother had to do it. As a result, unknown to them, I was dedicated to other gods while I was still in my mother's womb, and when I was born, other gods were thanked for my safe delivery. I was bound right from birth. I was born into an atmosphere where God was non-existent. The seven spirits of God were not in me, The spirit of the Lord, the spirit of understanding, fear of the Lord, counsel, might, wisdom, and of knowledge of the Lord. (Isa. 11:1-3) This means I was born completely blind to God and his works. My spirit was exposed to the spirits of evil. I was vulnerable right from the time I was conceived. My father had a very strong belief in ancestral spirits and believed they lead him in everything he did. Every morning he would put snuff in a wooden plate and prayed to his ancestors to protect him and the family and to look after him in his job. He had some cloth which he kept which the witch doctors had given him. It had red, white, and black colours and designs. He tied this around his neck like a scarf before putting a shirt on. It was triangular in shape and it was meant to look after him at work. When he got paid, he would put his money in a wooden plate and thanked the ancestors for giving him that money. Basically, I lived in a house where there was spiritual conflict: my mother by inviting church people to pray and in the same house my father worshipping his own gods. In the end, this fight manifested into the physical that they ended up separating. My father went to stay with another woman but my mother stayed looking after us and never remarried until her death. The word of the Lord says 'You shall have no other God besides me.' Deuteronomy 28:15-19 outlines the curses of disobedience.

> But if you refuse to listen to the Lord your God and do not obey all the commands and the decrees I am giving today, all these curses will come and overwhelm you. Your towns and fields will be cursed. Your baskets and breadboards will be cursed. Your children and your crops will be cursed. Wherever you go and whatever you do will be cursed (Duet. 28:15-19).

This means my parents were cut off from God's blessings and so was I. I was cursed because of the actions of my parents and my forefathers. I was bound, with curses of fruitless labour, poverty; my door was open to the devil, and that is why I ended up in a marriage in which I was abused. The evil spirits evoked by my father were monitoring my life and made sure that I got married to one who was never going to give me peace and love. If I tried to make money, I was financially abused; that money never amounted to anything, I had no peace, I was beaten up, and lost most of the things I worked for. This is fruitless labour. You work for something which you will never enjoy. All these attacks cause restlessness within your spirit and the devil is always happy to multiply distress in your life. Being in this situation causes stress, depression, mental instability, worrying, and no peace. All these are demons attacking your spirit, and they build up binding your spirit and locking it in. You are not free, you are bound. Demons are powerful, and in order to overcome, you need a stronger power in you. Jesus demonstrated that he is that power and that power was handed over to us Christians by Jesus himself when he said, 'I have been given all authority in the earth

A bound spirit is one that is united with demons. You can think of all evil spirits, spirit of murder, anxiety, depression, stress, poverty, lack, violence, prostitution, alcoholism, and many more. It is simply because the presence of the Lord is not there either through ignorance, your actions, or through the actions of your fathers and your forefathers. You always wonder why things are never right with you. Why everything gets messed up? The answer is so hidden. You can never suspect the actions of your father or your grandfathers to affect you. Lamech was affected by the actions of Cain generations after.

A bound marriage

When my husband wanted to marry me, his father had consulted some witch doctors to see if I would make him a good wife. On the other hand, at that time a ceremony to bring the dead back home was due to be done, and my father's family was preparing for that ceremony. Without any knowledge of where we were going or what we were doing, my father and his sisters took my brothers, my sister, and me to a place miles away from where we lived to consult a witch doctor. While we were there, my aunt asked if the man who wanted to marry me was a good man. The witch doctor said yes but I had to be dipped in the river early in the morning, like what is done in baptism. I had some incisions cut on my chest and some black powder rubbed in. In the early hours of the morning, when it was still dark, I was taken to the river by my aunts, and it was a big river with crocodiles and hippopotamus. I could see the hippopotamus in the distance as I was dipped in the water. My marriage was decided in the spiritual realms of the devil. It was never going to be one where joy and peace were to be experienced. It became a bound marriage, bound by the evil one who was now in charge of it. Now that I know God, I realise how people have messed my life and pray that God restores all the happiness lost and replaces all the bad things that have happened to me with good ones.

During our marriage, Cavin at one time got involved in witchcraft activity. The witchdoctor who was staying in his father's house, who Bev had accommodated told Cavin and his brother that there were things that needed to be done at their mother's grave. They were going to steal their mother's grave from her parent's farm where she was buried to their rural home. If they did this they were told, they would become rich. They had to go to the grave at night to avoid being seen by their mother's relatives. When they went, Cavin said,' as they approached the

grave, there was a smell like that of wet grain.' The witchdoctor told
them that it was the smell of a serpent that looked after the place. The
witchdoctor had to communicate with the serpent to get permission to
get to the grave. When they got to the grave, he said, there was some
struggling that occurred between the witchdoctor and the dead spirits at
the grave. The witchdoctor told them to throw some coins at the graves.
The struggles stopped then the witchdoctor said they had been allowed
to carry on with their proceedings. They killed a goat, and used its blood
to do some sacrifices. They then took, some soil from the grave and went
and buried it together with the goat's head at their rural home. This way,
the witchdoctor told them, they had moved the spirit of their mother
from where it was to their rural home to look after them.

The following night as they were leaving the village with the
witchdoctor, they missed the bus. They decided to walk to the main road
to do some hitch-hiking. As they were walking, they said that they heard
something that sounded like a bus and then people talking as if they had
alighted from a bus. In that area there had occurred a bus accident that
killed many people years back. One man wearing an overcoat and a hat
greeted them saying, 'Good evening.' The witchdoctor told them that the
man was one of their long dead relatives. Soon after, they saw hundreds of
people coming towards them, man, women and children. The witchdoctor
told them the people coming towards them were dead people and they
had to stick close to him as he started to speak in strange languages.
He said they walked past the people and none of them spoke a word to
them. I was in a marriage with a man who had gone to wake the dead,
perform sacrifices at graves and offer his money to the dead spirits. How
on earth were we going to prosper? What did it mean offering money at
graves and to awaken the dead? The devil is a liar. Their problems still
remained and even multiplied. This was seeking to be wealthy through
witchcraft means. As Christians, we give our tithes and offerings to the
Lord and God promises us prosperity and abundance. To whom were
Cavin and his brother offering their money to? They offered money at a
place of the dead. Remember the man possessed by demons lived in the
burial place. They took their money to the grave and so their prosperity

and abundance became buried there. They were never going to prosper because they had agreed to share with demons. God was looking, and he saw Cavin and his brother giving offerings to demons. In marriage you become one body. Being married to Cavin meant these actions were going to affect me and our children as well. God could not give me prosperity and abundance because of the partner I had. This explains my fruitlessness despite working hard. When he came home, how do I know that these spirits were not following him? He suffered mood swings, was never happy, very mean and violent. For days, Cavin was petrified about what he saw. He could not even go outside the house at night.

CHAPTER 9

The original spiritual man

The worst attack that the devil can have on a human being is the attack on his mind. It will cause man to forget about God and expose him to the evil spirits. The first thing the devil does is to convince man that he is better than God. He makes people believe in him and then he instils fear in people. But who is the devil in man's creation. He is never mentioned as being there in the beginning.

Genesis 1:26 *God said let us create human beings in our own image, to be like ourselves.* We hear that for everything else, God just said the word and whatever he said came to be. When he created man he consulted. He said let us, meaning he was talking to others. Colossians 1:15-16 says, *Christ is the visible image of the invisible God. He existed before anything was created and is supreme over all creation through him God created everything in heavenly realms and on earth.* Through Christ all things were created. Christ was there in the beginning, so God was talking to Christ. *The word was made flesh and dwelt among us.* John 1:14. So Christ is the son of the most high God; he is the Word of God. When he came to us, he came as the Word of God, and everything he spoke was exactly the Word of God coming to people and it was the power of God himself. It was God talking directly to people. When we speak the word, we are guaranteed the presence of God because it is Christ himself. The word is supreme over all creation. Everything else comes after the word. Through the word, things come to be in the spiritual realm first before it is manifested into the world.

Characteristics of the word:

- Active
- Authoritative
- Creative
- Powerful
- Loving
- Present on earth
- Holy
- It is God
- Anointed
- Accomplishes what it says
- Cannot be disputed
- Fights battles and always victors
- Cannot be blocked
- Knows no barriers
- Goes wherever it wants to go
- Heals disease
- Merciful trustworthy

The list is endless but one very amazing characteristic of the word is that it is spirit. When you read the bible, the word we read changes from its written form into spirit. It becomes active and alive accomplishing what it says. It becomes one with our spirit, enhancing our knowledge of God, strengthening our spirit and empowering our spirit to do as Christ did. The word has the power to bless, to change a person, to change situation, to protect and to fight battles because it alive and it is spiritual. We also know that the Holy Spirit was present as the word says, *in the beginning the Spirit of the lord was seen hovering over the water*. (Gen. 1:2) Characteristics of the Holy Spirit are the same as those of the word. It has no limitations. It is the power of God.

God's intention was for man to be like him, Christ, and the Holy Spirit. Therefore, God created man who had the same characteristics as him, Jesus Christ, and the Holy Spirit. God then created man and woman in the spiritual realm first. This was the original spirit man. He is the man that had no sin, the man who possessed God's holiness and purity. No sickness of any nature was with him, even mental illness. In order for God to put him on earth, he made shelter for him. This shelter, God moulded from dust, in his holy anointed hands, in his power and might. This shelter was clean, free of sin, faultless, pure, and holy. He breathed his spirit into this shelter we now call body. This he did to make sure that the spirit man would come directly from him with all the characteristics of God the Father, the Son, and the Holy Spirit. This is the spirit that was able to connect and to communicate with God. This is the spirit man God allowed to stand in his presence. God loved this man he had created so much that he provided him with everything and even trusted this spirit man to rule over all creation. When God creates a human being, it is first done in the spiritual realm as he says to Jeremiah in the first chapter of his book,' I have known you before I even formed you in your mother's womb and I ordained you.' This means Jeremiah had an assignment of which the training and ordination had already been performed before he was formed in his mother's womb. If we ask ourselves today, where did we come from? Yes, we can explain the flesh, but what about the spirit. In a newly born baby, if the spirit leaves, the baby is pronounced dead. The flesh would still be there but what about the spirit? It is the heavenly realms that we are first created and given names, training, and assignments. Adam and Eve were given their first assignment by God in the Garden of Eden. They were still in their sound minds. An attack of the mind is a way in which the devil makes us forget our assignments and our purpose on earth so that God's will for us is not accomplished. A person suffering from mental illness is never likely to accomplish God's assignment. God seeing that people were derailed by the devil and were failing to accomplish the tasks he had sent them to do, sent his son to restore man's spirit to its original state. It is not about the flesh but about the spirit. When God's spirit is in man, it is a unity of the father, the son, and the Holy Spirit. When the presence of God leaves, it is the whole presence of the trinity that leaves. Then the devil enters. He knows that the holy trinity is so powerful, so he also tries to make a strong unity in a person by driving in numerous demons. When a person is under demonic attack, it is never one spirit. The devil enters when we fail to subdue him. In 1 John 5:16, the word of the Lord says, 'We know that God's children do not make a practice of sinning, for God's son holds them securely and the evil one cannot touch them.'

An abuser is an agent for the devil

> Once you were dead because of your disobedience and your many sins. You used to live in sin just like the rest of the world, obeying the devil-the commander of the powers in the unseen world. He is the spirit at work in the hearts of those who do not obey God (Eph. 2:1-3).

An abuser is filled with evil spirits. Spirits that cause grief, pain, and suffering to mankind. They carry these spirits, transferring them into people they attack. One who was never angry becomes angry, one who had no grief becomes grieved. One who had happiness, becomes sorrowful, and one who had a free spirit, becomes tormented. In this day, we have got many abusers visiting churches. They come to pray with Christians yet they are carrying evil spirits in them and are abusing people including children of God. They are agents of the devil doing the devil's work. Many victims end up with mental health issues.

Paul talks about the spiritual bodies that leave the earth and return to the Father, when Jesus had said, the last words on the cross, it is written, 'His spirit left his body.' It is clear that the spirit of Jesus that was there in the beginning before the foundations of the earth had come to earth and was housed in a human body for the days it was on earth until his assignment had been completed. If Jesus had not subdued the devil, then his mission would not have been completed.

When God created us, he empowered us with his own spirit and with his fullness. Each one of us was sent to earth for a purpose but due to sin and attacks from the devil, we forget our assignments. The devil has attacked our knowledge, understanding, and the wisdom that God imparted in us that is why we forget. The devil targets our mind, thinking, understanding, and wisdom from God more than anything, for these lead us to our victory. He deceives us into disobeying God.

All hope is not gone

Saul is one person who disobeyed God. He was well known for persecuting Christians.

> Meanwhile, Saul was breathing out murderous threats against disciples. He went to the high priest and asked him for letters to the synagogues in Damascus so that if he found any there who belonged to the way, either man or women, he might take them as prisoners to Jerusalem (Acts 9:1).

In today's life, Saul would have been declared mentally ill, obsessed with persecuting and killing Christians and committing offences against humanity. In Cain's time, God would have cursed him and banished him from the land. The presence of God was not with him whatsoever. Saul was filled with hate, anger, and despised Christians. When the presence of God came upon him, he was completely delivered. All his sins were forgiven. We do not hear of him attending to any therapies or psychological input but the power which was in that light alone made a complete turn on his thinking and personality.

Colossians 2:9-10 'For in Christ lives all the fullness of God in human body. So you are also complete through your union with Christ, who is the head over every ruler and authority.'

After receiving Christ as my Lord, something happened that shocked my father's family. My grandmother, (my father's mum) had passed away, and there was a memorial service for her. As I lived far away from her at that time, I could not make it for the funeral, so I had to go for her memorial service. The service was done in the day. At night, unknown to us, my uncle had invited two men he called prophets. We were all called to one room. One of my aunts was severely ill and was expected to die any time. One of the so-called prophets looked at me and asked what church I went to and I told him. He started criticising me and the church I went to. He asked me to sit next to my sick aunt. He lit two candles and put them in front of us. He started to pray, and the moment he tried to touch my head, the power of God came on me so strong. I immediately went into tongues. I could feel the power of God all over me. The man couldn't touch my head; he was lifted high up into the air from his standing position, and turned, legs in the air and head towards the floor. He came down and his head hit the cement floor so hard and with a loud bang. He crouched and started running like a monkey climbing trees and leaping from tree to tree. Everyone panicked, and they went out, looking for him with torches. I didn't panic but instead I started singing praises to the Lord while others were running around. It turned out later that these men were witch doctors and were lying that they were man of God so that all family members who had gathered would accept them. They had wanted to transfer what my aunt was suffering from to me through witch craft activity. Jesus in me would not allow it.

CHAPTER 10

Rebirth of the spirit

The angel of the Lord speaking to Mary

> The Holy Spirit will come upon you and the power of the
> highest will overshadow you, therefore, also that holy one who
> is to be born will be called The Son of God (Luke 1:35).

The angel of the Lord speaks to Mary, explaining how she was going to become pregnant. This marked the beginning of how each one of us was going to be redeemed from sin and be acceptable before God. The spirit of God was going to overshadow Mary, and she was going to have a son. Anyone born of the Holy Spirit becomes a child of the Holy Spirit. This is the pattern that was going to follow. Every one of us who believes in God and Jesus Christ that he died for our sins and rose on the third day would be born again but this time of the Spirit of God. The Holy Spirit will overshadow them that believe and drive out what is not of God. The Holy Spirit will fill them with a new spirit who is the true identity of God the Father, Jesus the Son, and the Holy Spirit as it was in the beginning.

He gave us the right to become children of God, those who believe in his name, who were born not of blood nor of flesh, nor the will of man but God (John 1:12).

Being born again is when the spirit of God overshadows man as it did with Mary but this time does not make man pregnant. Instead, all sin is taken away and the Holy Spirit comes in as a new the spirit man who is the original man created by God in the beginning. This spirit man leaves the human body when man sins against God. This spiritual man is the presence of God in man. The spirit man can only be restored by confessing your sins and confessing with your mouths that Jesus is the Lord and saviour of your life, that he died and resurrected, and allowing him to come and live in you.

We understand that God is a spirit and anyone who is born of the spirit is spirit. Jesus was full of power and authority because in his human body dwelt the spirit of God, power, glory, authority, and might. This is the power that had authority over the disease, sickness, and evil spirits. It is the same spirit that resurrected the dead, and it is the same spirit that preached the gospel and performed many miracles. Paul says our earthly bodies die and is buried in the ground. (1 Cor. 15) They are only meant to be shelter and nothing more. Our bodies are only shelter for our spirits when we are on this earth. Like houses, it is either the house is inhabited by a good person or by a bad person. A house can be accommodated by a priest, a pastor, a prostitute, a thief, or a murderer. Now that is the same with our bodies. It is either they are sheltering a good spirit man or a bad spirit man. When either of the spirits, good or bad, leaves the body, then the use of the body as shelter seizes to function. A body carrying bad spirit is the one that is cut off from God due to disobedience but still has chance for restoration through Jesus Christ. The evil spirits in man have no inheritance in the kingdom of God; they are destined for hell while the good spirit man will inherit all the promises of God. Jesus came to make right every spirit and restore the presence of God to everyone. This presence of God does not die even in death of the body but carries on to live in the kingdom of God where it originated from.

When the presence of God enters the body, the presence of the devil leaves. This is how a miracle is received. Mental illness is a disease like any other disease, and Jesus healed all disease. Matthew 4:24 says *and whatever sickness or disease or if they were demon possessed or epileptic or paralysed, he healed them all.*

A place in Jesus

The word of the Lord says we live in Jesus and he lives in us. The spirit of *Jesus* is enough for every heart that seeks him. Where the presence of Jesus is, the presence of the God the Father and the Holy Spirit is also there. The presence of Jesus is never without the presence of God. It fills the whole earth. When a relationship is made between Jesus and a person, that means a person's spirit becomes intertwined with Jesus' spirit. In John 18:21-23 Jesus prays and says,

I pray that they will all be one, just as you and I are one-as you are in me, Father, and I am in you. And may they be in us that the world may believe you send me. I have given them the glory you gave me, so they may be one as we are one. I am in them as you are in me. May they experience such perfect unity that the world will know that you send me and you love them as much as you love me.

His spirit is united with the fathers. It is one with God and Jesus; therefore, the person's spirit becomes intertwined with that of God the Father, Jesus the Son, and the Holy Spirit. The spirits are united and become one. The person now lives in God's protection and power. David says, 'The Lord is my rock and my refuge. In him I find shelter. He hides me in his feathers. David is explaining how close he is to God. He is in this place where nothing can harm or get close to him. And Paul says *we are seated in Jesus Christ above all the powers and principalities of darkness.* Jesus is a place of shelter, love, security, authority, provision, and comfort. This place is huge and accommodates all who want to be in it. It is a place of honour.

When I visited Bev in our house, the house that she has now claimed as hers. Cavin and I had come from my mother's memorial service, and we were going to stay there for the night. Bev made a place for us to sleep. She put a double bed mattress on a single bed base so that the mattress was overlapping on both sides. When I saw it, I just thought to myself, how someone can sleep on a bed like that, they will roll over and fall. So I took the mattress of the bed and made our bed on the floor. Cavin was talking to his brother but I was tired and wanted to rest. I said my prayer and then said Psalm 91, my favourite. As soon as I finished saying it and said amen, a flash of light shone under the base of the bed where we were going to sleep. Something slid under the bed and stopped right where I could see it. It was a wooden plate curved on the sides. It looked like the one my father used but this one had some writings on it. On top of it was two swords like knives, with carvings on, and these were neatly arranged, crossing one another on top of the wooden plate. I knew this was some sort of witchcraft which God had exposed. I prayed and sprinkled everything with the blood of Jesus and bind everything in Jesus' name. After praying, the spirit of the Lord asked me to call the owner to come and take his/her things. I called Cavin and showed him; he was petrified but I felt bold in myself. The spirit of the Lord was upon me. His brother who also had moved into this house came and said, 'These are mine. They are not meant to hurt anybody. They are not harmful.' If they are not harmful, then what are these things and what are they meant to do.? Why keep them? For what use are you keeping them? In the early hours of the morning when I finished my early morning prayer, a mighty wind blew over the house with a great and terrifying noise. It sounded as if the rooftop was going to be blown off. When it finished, a huge black and white cock was found hanging mysteriously dead on the fence of the chicken run. That chicken was cooked, and I was given to eat but I just turned around and said the word of the Lord does not allow me to eat an animal they die of natural causes. My friend and prayer partner Neddy visited me the following day and said, 'What happened at your house last night? I had a dream, there were so many people interceding there and one of them was a huge man sitting in the heavenly realms interceding as well.' I knew God had done it again. He had come to my rescue for the weapon that was formed against me had been conqured.

All who worship idols will be disgraced along with all their craftsmen, mere humans who claim they can make a God.

The blacksmith stands at the forge to make a sharp tool, pounding and shaping it with all his might. His work makes him hungry and weak.

> The wood carver measures a block of wood and draws a pattern
> on it. He works with a chisel and plane and curves it into a
> human figure. He gives it human beauty and puts it in a little
> shrine (Isa. 44:11-13).

God is showing us that he is the one who created the wood, the iron, and the man who makes idols; therefore, how can these idols have power over God. The same tree he gave life, watered through rain is the same tree that people use for firewood, for furniture, and then a piece is cut out of it to make a God. The carver needs strength to complete his task. All these have no power over God. When the devil uses these things, he can never have power above that of God. I understood the magnitude of the power of God the Father, Jesus, and the Holy Spirit that I had accepted in my life. That's why in Isaiah 54:17 the Lord says, 'No weapon formed against you shall prosper.'

The blood of Jesus

The blood of Jesus is powerful. It is our hope and our future. It is the blood that washes our sins. (1John 1:7) This blood is spiritual like the Holy Spirit. So when we speak the blood, it is right there. It fills the whole earth, and reaches to every place. It does not matter where you are or what situation you are in, the blood of Jesus knows no limits and has no boundaries. It is always available.

The weapons of war

As Christians, we have weapons that God has given us to use in our fight. In order to destroy all the altars that my life had been dedicated to, I learnt how to use some of the weapons to tackle the giants in my path.

> We are humans but we do not wage war as humans do. We use
> God's mighty weapons, not worldly weapons to knock down

strongholds of human reasoning and destroy false arguments
(Cor. 10:4).

The weapons are divine and supernatural. The Bible tells us about some of them. Include them in prayers. Sent them to fight, bind, arrest, and attack the enemy. I have used them and they work. The enemy is the devil and the powers of darkness.

The Holy Spirit is always there to fight on our behalf. He sees what we cannot see and hear's what we cannot hear. He guides us out of trouble.

> The name of Jesus
> The blood of Jesus
> Fire of God
> Stone of David
> Shield and sword of the Holy Spirit
> The stuff of Moses

And everything else that men and women of God used in their battles. These weapons are still alive and are there for our use as long as we use it in the name of Jesus. These are the same weapons that the devil copies and uses but his weapons can never have more power than the weapons of God.

The altar of the Lord is the place for receiving blessings. Before Abram received his blessing, he built God an altar.(Genesis 12:7) Gideon was instructed by God to first destroy his father's altar and build one for God. (Judges 6:25-26)Then the blessing followed. It is important to pull down all the ancestral and satanic altars controlling your life through prayer. Tear apart every idol God controlling your life and build your own alter of God in your spirit.

I thank Jesus for dying for me on the cross. Colossians 1:13 says, 'For he rescued me from the kingdom of darkness and transferred me into the kingdom of his dear son who purchased my freedom and forgave my sins.'

And now I am convinced that nothing can separate us from the love of God. Neither death, nor life, neither angels nor demons, neither fears from today nor our worries about tomorrow-not even the powers of hell can separate us from God's love. No power in the sky above or the earth below, indeed nothing in all creation will ever be able to separate us from the love of God that is revealed in Christ Jesus our Lord (Rom. 8:38-39).

I forgive all the people who have played part in making my life unbearable. May the light of the Lord find them and redeem them from their sins.

Glory be to God forever and ever.

CONCLUSION

I discovered that Cavin was cheating on me. He had arranged that his mistress stay with Bev in the house that I had worked for. Cavin and I are separated and now I am still waiting for him to sign divorce papers.

BIBLIOGRAPHY

Bill Wiese, *23 Minutes in Hell.* Spiritlessons.com.

Emmanuel Eni, *Delivered from the Powers of Hell.* Spiritlessons.com.

ABOUT THE AUTHOR

Margret David, born the second child out of six, had a normal happy childhood. She qualified as a teacher and later on as a nurse. Margret is a Christian, a member of the intercession group, and a member of the women fellowship. Margret has also enjoyed preaching in her church.

INDEX

www.ingramcontent.com/pod-product-compliance
Lightning Source LLC
Chambersburg PA
CBHW020346290526
45785CB00005B/2169